The Beginner's Guide to Becoming a Better Basketball Player

The Beginner's Guide to Becoming a Better Basketball Player

Contents

INTRODUCTION 8
SOME BASKETBALL HISTORY 14
TYPES OF BASKETBALL ORGANIZATIONS 18
HIGH SCHOOL BASKETBALL CAMPS..22
BASKETBALL ACADEMY BENEFITS 25
WRITING FIRST BASKETBALL LETTER 27
SAMPLE LETTER TO COLLEGE BASKETBALL COACHES........................30
10,000 HOURS RULE: BEGINNER TO EXPERT 322
MONDAY THROUGH FRIDAY WORKOUT PLAN 344
MONDAY (SHOOTING AND LIFTING) WORKOUT 366
TUESDAY (DRIBBLING AND LIFTING) WORKOUT......................................44
WEDNESDAY (PASSING WITH A LITTLE SHOOTING) WORKOUT 51
THURSDAY (DEFENSE WITH A LITTLE SHOOTING) WORKOUT 53
FRIDAY (CONDITIONING WITH A LITTLE SHOOTING & LIFTING) WORKOUT 56
MONDAY-FRIDAY CONDITIONING & WEIGHTLIFTING WORKOUT 61
NOTES/TIPS 66
CONCLUSION...67
RESOURCES 68

2

The Beginner's Guide to Becoming a Better Basketball Player

Copyright © 2014 by Lamar Hull

Published: 18th July 2014

Publisher: Lamar Hull

This book is basketball related with real-life stories and inspiration. All rights reserved. Except as permitted under the US Copyright Act of 1976, no part of this publication may be reproduced, distributed, or transmitted in any form or by any means, or stored in a database or retrieval system, without prior consent of the Author.

I'd like to dedicate this eBook to: my beautiful wife Tamisha, without her encouragement, this eBook would have not been created; my children Madison, Blake and Carter who continue to drive my passion in life; my grandma and grandpa (R.I.P.), for teaching me the values of life and raising me to be a respectable person; my mom (R.I.P.) and dad, who brought me in to this world; the rest of my family that believed in me; Coach Mckillop for giving me the opportunity to play at Davidson College; Sean Kilmartin for helping me fulfill my dreams of playing professional basketball overseas; Ric Elias for being a great mentor and last but not least; God who continues to give me faith in HIM and everything that I do.

Lamar currently coaches a 6th grade AAU team. Lamar Hull works in the Search Engine Optimization industry, helping optimize and rank websites in the search results. Lamar has a youth basketball website that inspires young players to follow their dreams. Inspirational Basketball is a great basketball resource for players, coaches and parents. Visit his website at *http://inspirationalbasketball.com/*.

The Beginner's Guide to Becoming a Better Basketball Player

"I admire Lamar tremendously because I've seen firsthand his work ethic and desire to be great despite any hurdle. My 1 on 1 partner from day 1 at Davidson, he pushed me to better myself and this story tells why."

- Stephen Curry, *NBA Player*, Golden State Warriors

"Lamar has a tremendous passion for basketball. He was an excellent basketball player and is now one of the most dedicated coaches I've ever met!"

- Ben Allison, Former *Davidson College Player* and Professional Basketball Player, and author of Reach the Rim

---

"It's no secret why Lamar Hull's basketball career at Davidson was a story of team success and personal development. Lamar had a magnificent attitude that always put team ahead of self. He came to practice every day with the intent and work ethic to push his teammates to make them better. In the process, he himself became a better player and a better teammate. Lamar's attitude contributed significantly to the incredible collective success that he and his teammates experienced and enjoyed during his time in a Davidson uniform."

- Bob Mckillop, *Head Coach,* Davidson College

"I have had the pleasure of coaching, training, and playing alongside Lamar on a few occasions and when you talk about committed, that would be an understatement. Lamar has and continues to sacrifice his own time and time away from his family to inspire and develop the youth of our next generation as a coach and mentor."

- Marlon Garnett, *Former NBA Player, Celtics*, and Coach of Team Garnett Basketball

"For many years I have admired Lamar's incredible work ethic and desire to become a better basketball coach. Moreover, the lives that will be impacted by what he will achieve by writing a book about his life lessons."

- Lawrence Gordon, AAU Coach, Southern Kings, *coached Randolph Morris (KU), Tony Parker (UCLA) and more*

"Lamar is one of the most inspiring and determined individuals that I know. I have never met anyone in my lifetime with such drive and perseverance. He strives to be the best at whatever he sets his mind to. With all of these attributes, Lamar has left behind an illustrious basketball career and is determined to instill every ounce of his knowledge in to the next generation of young basketball players. Lamar is also a devoted husband and father and I am glad to call him family!"

- Lamont Reid, *WCU Football All-American,* All-Pro AFL and former NFL running back

---

"Lamar's desire to get better at everything he does make him a great role model especially for young people. Having worked and coached with Lamar for a number of years has shown me the kind of person he is. Anyone that associates with him will benefit from his tremendous drive and kind heart. I can't wait to see what his life's journey has in store for him."

- Ric Elias, *CEO* of Red Ventures

"Lamar Hull is the epitome of perseverance. He never takes "No" for an answer. He came to practice every day, ready to work and push his teammates to be better because he knew that's what it took for the team to succeed. His dedication is an inspiration to everyone around him."

- Kenny Grant, *Professional Basketball Player* for SLUC Nancy Basket in France

The Beginner's Guide to Becoming a Better Basketball Player

"During my junior year, Lamar was a senior and we were roommates, we became brothers on and off the court. I have so many memories to only pick one, but I remember and miss our talks after a good or bad game. I remember how he was always such a work horse and pushed me to try harder. I wish we could have played on the same team overseas, how fun would that have been?

- Boris Meno, Professional Basketball Player for Aix Maurienne, France

"Lamar was tremendously competitive as a player and he has taken that competitiveness and passion for the game of basketball and made himself a terrific teacher and coach."

- Dino Gaudio, *ESPN Basketball Analysts*, and former Head Coach of Wake Forest

"Lamar is a truly inspiring player and person. He overcame many obstacles to get where he did in his basketball career. He epitomizes the traits that every player and coach wants on their team - toughness, positive attitude, great work ethic, high basketball IQ and others. It's not surprising to me that Lamar is where he's at today as he has used these same characteristics to become very successful off the court!"

- Brendan Winters, *Co-founder and Coach* of Pro Skills Basketball

The Beginner's Guide to Become a Better Basketball Player

Lamar Hull

http://inspirationalbasketball.com/

inspirationalbasketball20@gmail.com

The Beginner's Guide to Becoming a Better Basketball Player

Introduction

"The game of basketball has been everything to me. My place of refuge, place I've always gone where I needed comfort and peace. It's been the site of intense pain and the most intense feelings of joy and satisfaction. It's a relationship that has evolved over time, given me the greatest respect and love for the game."

– Michael Jordan

My name is Lamar Hull, and this is my basketball story. What makes it different from other inspirational stories is my dedication of perseverance, discipline and hard-work ethic. I grew up in a North Carolina town of about 1,500 people where football was such a dominant sport; the town was dubbed "The Biggest Smallest Football Town in the World." One area of my town, although populated by low-income families, had a reputation of producing great athletes, although there were just as many, if not more athletes who halted their careers after high school. Perhaps because of this, or perhaps because they wanted me to be as well-rounded as possible, my grandparents raised me with a strict focus on manners, academics and God. It wasn't until I finished my own journey that I was able to understand everything in hindsight.

Basketball caught my eye immediately, despite the abundance of football mania in town, because of one park that drew crowds of more than fifty players and spectators each Sunday. I was hesitant to join in because of my small size and young age, so I started by watching from the sidelines and formulating a plan on how I could become better than the players that were actually playing. One of my first inspirations and motivations came from "Pistol" Pete Maravich, whose story made such an impression on me that I immediately ordered his homework basketball drills. I started slowly: two hours each day were spent on passing, shooting, dribbling and ball-handling respectively.

The Beginner's Guide to Becoming a Better Basketball Player

Soon, my strengths and weaknesses presented themselves. While I excelled in ball-handling, my lack of consistent shooting meant I was missing game-winning free throws for my AAU team, the Newton Flames. No matter how quick I was or that I could break a full-court press by myself, it was evident that I had to work on my shooting and so I returned to the drawing board. I quickly needed some instance offense. This time, I refocused my plan around Steve Nash's shooting drills and spent half of my workout time at the local recreation center working on shooting alone. Going as far as I could with basketball as my passion, I put as much effort and dedication into it as I could. I even slept with my basketball at night! I wanted to succeed at basketball as badly as I wanted to breathe. I put myself through my own weekly training program and it paid off.

By middle school, my goal was to make one of the four spots available to seventh graders on the basketball team - a daunting task, considering how many of my friends and classmates were good at basketball. I ended up making the team but spent a lot of time on the bench as the older kids were awarded more playing time. Instead of being upset about this, I used it as an opportunity to learn about basketball etiquette, such as wearing a suit and tie to all the away games. Looking ahead to where I am at now, this experience showed me how to be professional whether I was playing basketball for a living or working in a corporate environment. I also found that the mental and physical toughness that I'd acquired in football had transferred to the basketball court. So, if any parents are reading this and you have asked the question, are there any benefits for your child playing multiple sports, the answer is yes! I started to notice that I loved physical contact, so I spent a lot of my time at the free-throw line. I wasn't afraid to drive inside against the giants and get 'And-1s'.

Being an AAU player left me with many great memories, like the time I squared off against current-NBA player Chris Paul and finished the game with twenty-six points to his twenty-seven. Playing against someone of Chris's caliber made me realize that I could play with any player in the nation; those types of situations encouraged me to dig deeper and work even harder. AAU is a lot different from what it used to be, but AAU still provides a great opportunity for young players to excel and be noticed.

The Beginner's Guide to Becoming a Better Basketball Player

The basketball coach at my high school had heard about me and invited me to practice with the varsity team, even though I was only a freshman. The upperclassmen were not happy when I kept breaking their presses and scoring on them, but I was there to both make them and myself better. To gain experience, I played and dominated Junior Varsity and was then called up to play Varsity near the end of the season heading into the playoffs. Scoring an average of twenty-five points a game as a freshman on Junior Varsity, turned me into a leader and allotted me more playing time when others got hurt on the Varsity team.

One person who helped me immensely was my older brother, especially during my sophomore year. While I was only five foot eight inches, he had five inches on me and seeing him being heavily recruited by top schools motivated me to push through to another level. It was because of this, that I also began to understand why my town had so many seemingly great athletes that fizzled.

The Beginner's Guide to Becoming a Better Basketball Player

They had all the talent in the world, but few of them were willing to put in the countless hours it took to become a collegiate or professional athlete. There was also a disregard for academics, something, which went directly against everything my grandparents had taught me. Keeping their message in my mind, I brought my schoolwork with me to games and worked through it in between games before it was my turn to play. Doing it this way meant I had fewer distractions and as a result, I graduated fifth in my class with a four point one GPA and as the Beta Club Vice President, the Science Club president, the Leo Club president and as a Varsity Program member. To further challenge myself, I took all Advanced Placement courses during my senior year to bolster my chances of being able to go to a good college.

I didn't have much of an idea on how recruitment worked, so I created my own method. Grab a pencil and take notes, here is my quick guide to earning a basketball scholarship. I *drafted a letter outlining my skills,* achievements and interests and then sent it to every head and assistant coach I had an interest in playing for. Although I received a response from every one of them, only a few of them had the recruiting flexibility for me. Clemson University's head coach Larry Shyatt and staff showed interest in me after watching one of my teammates play. My teammate was a 6'8" freshman and that's all he had to be. After witnessing me carry the load on offense and defense, they were very interested in me playing for the Clemson Tigers. After all, Clemson was known for recruiting small guards. On March 17th, 2003, Coach Shyatt resigned as the head coach of the men's basketball program. My basketball dreams were temporarily shattered.

My goal now was to visit as many schools as possible. The one that seemed like the best fit for me was Davidson College; this was based on the small class size, types of courses, and basketball staff. I knew that playing in the NBA was probably not the reality, but Coach McKillop's connections to overseas basketball leagues piqued my interest. After acing my SAT and receiving an acceptance letter to Davidson, I suffered a setback when I was cut from the team in my first year. Imagine all the hard-work, time and commitment to the game of basketball.

The Beginner's Guide to Becoming a Better Basketball Player

I felt like it was all worth nothing, as I knew I could help the Davidson team. I was so distraught that I briefly considered quitting college. I thought about all the hard work on the basketball court and what I wanted to accomplish in life, I felt like a failure.

Through the grace of God and my faith, I dusted myself off instead, gathered my thoughts, and worked so hard that I made the team the next year. I was off to a roaring start, only to encounter another obstacle when I became injured and had to sit out the second half of the season. I was definitely used to adversity by now; I rehabbed carefully and came back to the team in my third year, making a nothing-but-net three-pointer at the buzzer. What a rush! However, I'd focused so intensely on sports that I neglected my studies and had to sit out the second half to pull up my grades. I was so disappointed in myself, but I channeled that into determination and did everything I could do to better myself in sports and academics so that I'd be ready for my senior year. I was fortunate enough to have a great group of teammates (Kenny Grant, Boris Meno, Brendan Winters and others) to encourage me through the rough times.

My last year at Davidson was pretty magical. I got to play with Stephen Curry, a current NBA superstar that I beat one-on-one and will not let him forget it until this day. I know better than to try and play him now. After my senior season, I was academically ready to graduate that spring with a degree in Biology. I was a little unsure of where to go after that and seemed torn between two dreams: becoming a pharmacist, and playing basketball professionally. Because of the unselfish and persevering attitude I'd shown playing for Davidson, Coach Mckillop made a call to a good friend of his on my behalf and before I knew it, I was on a plane across the Atlantic Ocean to play in the coastal town of Kings Lynn, England.

The Beginner's Guide to Becoming a Better Basketball Player

The USA Select Basketball program helps basketball players fulfill their dream of playing basketball professionally overseas. Because of Coach Mckillop's connection with Sean Kilmartin and the USA Select Basketball Program, I signed a professional basketball contract overseas. I was on a ten hour flight and had no time to rest: my first game was that night, and I was happy to see that Englanders both loved basketball and Americans who could play the game. My teammates and opponents included Davidson alumni and graduates from other colleges, and I finally got the opportunity to dominate and show my potential in games, which is something I hadn't had the chance to do while at Davidson. Oh yeah, and the money wasn't too shabby, either.

I led the league in points, assists and steals as a point guard during my first year that I played in England, and even though I received contractual offers to play at higher levels, I had what I felt was a more important duty: raising a beautiful daughter. So, I made the tough decision to end my basketball career and focus on being a parent and giving back to the basketball community for all it had given me. You can now find me helping fulfill children's dreams by teaching them basketball tips and drills on my website, Inspirational Basketball.

The Beginner's Guide to Becoming a Better Basketball Player

Thank you for reading my story, and I hope it helps you on your journey towards achieving your basketball dreams similar to the way that I achieved mine. I also wanted to add, that the journey won't be easy, but how bad do you want it? Will you wake up every day and maximize the opportunity to get better? To paraphrase motivational speaker [Eric Thomas's "Secret to Success" video](); to reach success, you'll have to give it everything you've got: when you want to succeed as bad as you want to breathe, then you will be successful. This applies to anything in life, not just basketball. I came from a community where I didn't have all the cool gadgets or money. With my small stature and skill set that wasn't typical of a basketball player, I achieved my dream because I had a lot of perseverance, determination, hard-work and discipline. You'll encounter many obstacles and challenges along the way, but if you just keep your eye on the finish line, nothing can get in your way. **So, my question to you, yes I'm talking to you, how bad do you want it? What will you give up to accomplish your dreams?**

SOME BASKETBALL HISTORY

"There is winning and there is losing and in life both will happen. What is never acceptable to me is quitting."

– Magic Johnson

The game of basketball was invented in 1891 by Dr. James Naismith at the YMCA in Springfield, Massachusetts. Searching for a way to keep the students in the gym class, he came up with the idea of nailing peach baskets to a ten-foot elevated track, divided the students into two teams, and instructed them to place the ball into the peach basket on the opposite side from where they started to play. Shortly after, he recognized the inefficiency of taking the ball out of the basket each time and removed the bottom for increased flow of the game.

After only four years, the game's popularity meant it spread to the high school level with women primarily playing, and the first college boasting of the sport was Pittsburgh Geneva College, inaugurated by Naismith's colleague, C.O. Beamis. The sport continued to spread to other colleges and the first intercollegiate game was played that year with the host school Hamline University losing to University of Minnesota-affiliated School of Agriculture, nine to three. The first time the game was played in Canada was in 1904 when Kingston, Ontario's Queen's University hosted McGill University of Montreal Quebec; the visitors won nine to seven in a ten-minute overtime after both teams finished regulation time tied seven to seven.

In 1906, the peach baskets had been replaced with metal hoops against a backboard so the ball could fall through more easily with one point still being awarded for each successful attempt. Just forty-eight years after the game's inception, its first men's national championship tournament was held, and the first official National Collegiate Athletic Association (NCAA) championship tournament followed two years after in 1939.

The Beginner's Guide to Becoming a Better Basketball Player

The first professional basketball association, the Basketball Association of America (BAA) was founded in 1946 but merged with the National Basketball League after only three years to form what is now known as the National Basketball Association (NBA). There were originally seventeen teams in its first year, shrinking to eleven the next, and down to just eight in 1953, all of which are still teams in today's league. The first expansion occurred in 1961 with the Chicago Packers (today's Washington Wizards) joining the league; the first major expansion, with another five teams joining (Chicago Bulls, Seattle SuperSonics, Oklahoma City Thunder today, San Diego- Houston- Rockets, Milwaukee Bucks and Phoenix Suns), occurred in 1968. By 1974, the Portland Trail Blazers, Cleveland Cavaliers, Buffalo Braves (Los Angeles Clippers) and New Orleans- Utah- Jazz had brought the total number of teams to eighteen.

Two years passed before another four teams became part of the NBA: San Antonio Spurs, Denver Nuggets, Indiana Pacers and New York (Brooklyn) Nets. Expansion slowed after that with several years elapsing before the Dallas Mavericks became the league's newest team. However, this lull in activity wouldn't last long and by 1988-89, the Charlotte Hornets, Miami Heat, Orlando Magic and Minnesota Timberwolves caused the teams to now number twenty-seven. Expansion to Canada occurred in 1995 with the Toronto Raptors and Vancouver Grizzlies; however, the latter lasted only six years before being relocated to Memphis, still retaining the Grizzlies name.

Professional basketball took much longer to expand to an all-women's league, but in 1996, one year after the last expansion, the Women's National Basketball Association was formed with eight teams, each one being associated to a team in the NBA. In 1998-99, four more teams were added to the league and only one year later, another four joined to bring the number up to sixteen, twice its original number of teams. However, a sale in 2002 meant that two teams, the Miami Sol and Portland Fire, became defunct because nobody bought them, lowering the number of teams in the WNBA to fourteen.

The Beginner's Guide to Becoming a Better Basketball Player

The Cleveland Rockers followed suit a year later, but in 2006, a team was awarded to Chicago (the Sky) and brought the number up teams back up to fourteen. One more folding-and-expansion occurred in 2006-2007 (Charlotte Sting; Atlanta Dream) with a final two teams folding due to lack of ownership (Houston Comets, Sacramento Monarchs) in 2008 and 2009, respectively. This was for those of us who are truly passionate about basketball; you can't know where you are going, if you don't know the history. That is an old saying that my grandparents taught me. **Do you know your basketball history? Are you passionate about your dream in all aspects?**

The Beginner's Guide to Becoming a Better Basketball Player

TYPES OF BASKETBALL ORGANIZATIONS

"Some people want it to happen, some people wish it would happen, others make it happen."

-Michael Jordan

In my personal story, I talked about how I got the opportunity to play with current NBA player Chris Paul. We played a game together and I ended up scoring only one point less than he did - something I'm pretty proud of, considering Chris's stock in the NBA right now. I really enjoyed playing AAU, partly because of the intensity and because of the players I was exposed to. The Amateur Athletic Union and Youth Basketball of America are two great roads to travel on when you want to pursue your passion, but it may not necessarily be for everyone. In this section, I'll talk about some of the pros and cons associated with each group.

Amateur Athletic Union

[AAU](#) is an organization dedicated to helping athletes of many sports and age levels to pursue their dreams. There are about half a million kids who belong to this non-profit organization. Here are some of the points I feel are good and bad about it:

Pros

- The sheer size of the organization means that there are plenty of resources, such as good income flow and an abundance of coaches and professionals. The more a group can take care of the business side, the more secure it is and can spend most of its time dedicated to helping athletes.

- With thirty-thousand age division events, there is no shortage of stages in which you can compete. Whether you're playing a popular sport like basketball or a lesser-known

18

one like power-lifting, there is plenty of competition for you that you may not get in an ordinary house or rep league.

- The AAU has world-class athletic facilities, so you get used to playing in professional venues at a much earlier age. It's one thing to shoot hoops at a rundown court after school; it's another thing altogether to have a full-sized hardwood court with regulation nets.

- AAU has three divisions, so there are three tier levels of competition. AAU I typically has the most talented teams but is not limited to this division.

Cons

- The competition can be pretty fierce. If you're the type of person who works better with gentler coaching and being able to work at your own pace, you might not find it here. Also, it can be a little intimidating trying to play your best against future star professional athletes.

- AAU has been hit with a couple of scandals, perhaps making potential members doubt the true interest of the league.

- Traveling to all the games and tournaments may be a bit of a financial burden for some athletes. The very best competition is likely not going to be found within bus or driving distance of your city, and having to trek it to all corners of the country may be a little hard.

Youth Basketball of America

This is another American organization that focuses on developing sports for children and teens, but with a focus solely on basketball. Because its focus is centered on only one sport, some of the pros and cons associated with the [YBOA](#) are a little different. One thing to consider, YBOA is perceived as less competitive than AAU.

Pros

- They have tournaments in a variety of states across the country, so finding a high-intensity way to play is always an option that's not too far from where you live.

- You can order uniforms especially from them, giving your team a more uniform look (pun intended). The YBOA also offers car rental discounts, so for you or your parents, finding your way around a foreign city is much more comfortable than having to go at it by bus.

Cons

- Although they have tournaments in many states, the YBOA doesn't have tournaments in every state. This may mean that travel is much harder for some players than others, and you might have to give up valuable playing time in favor of life's necessities.

- Their summer basketball camps are both in Orlando, Florida, as opposed to other organizations holding them in various cities across the country. If you live in California or Oregon, these camps may not be the easiest to attend for you.

- Instead of just straight up joining the organization, you find someone willing to coach a team and enough players (up to twelve) to fill a roster. If you don't know a coach and eleven other players, finding a spot on the team is that much harder.

The Beginner's Guide to Becoming a Better Basketball Player

These are just a few pros and cons about each organization that I hope give you a better understanding of which one you or your player should consider joining. The best thing you can do is to find people who are a part of one or both and talk to them, or even call up the organizations themselves and speak to someone who works there. They'll be able to answer all your questions because they work there, have the most up-to-date and accurate information, and can help you figure out if either organization is a fit for you. Whichever path you take, facing off against the most talented, skilled and disciplined players is one of the best ways to improve your game. Other people may not agree with me 100%, I'm just giving my honest feedback!

The Beginner's Guide to Becoming a Better Basketball Player

High School Basketball Camps

"I've missed more than 9,000 shots in my career. I've lost almost 300 games. 26 times, I've been trusted to take the game-winning shot, and missed. I've failed over and over and over again in my life. And that is why I succeed."

- Michael Jordan

I went to a regular high school in a regular town in North Carolina. Being surrounded by many football athletes, I had to seek out my own basketball training regimen - not an easy task. Had I had the opportunity to go to a basketball camp during my high school years, I would have jumped at the chance. The idea of being surrounded by other players who were just as serious and disciplined about the sport as I was is something I wish I could have done. Unfortunately, it wasn't in the cards for me but I've compiled a list of basketball camps that may work for you. To break it down, I've organized them according to geography in the U.S.

Pacific Northwest: NBC Camps in La Grande, Oregon is a good place for high school students living in Oregon, Washington, Idaho, Alaska and California as you can select from a number of different types of camps. You'll spend two weeks there surrounded by three-hundred athletes as they teach you about building and strengthening your decision making skills on and off the court. The Rip City Basketball Academy is another camp, offering up players the chance to work intensely on their basketball skills.

Pacific Southwest: PGC Basketball is a huge organization, running camps all across the U.S. In the Pacific Southwest, you can find camps in Oklahoma and Texas, two states, which have highly competitive NBA teams in the Thunder and Spurs. In Southern California, SoCal Hoops offers a series of camps for students living a little more north of the previous camps.

The Beginner's Guide to Becoming a Better Basketball Player

Rocky Mountain States: In Fort Collins, Colorado, the Rocky Mountain Basketball Camp holds summer camps for aspiring basketball players in a number of different age categories. Despite only being in their sixth year, this camp is all about improving on your skills while also building character at the same time. Elite League Basketball, with their motto being, "One week is not enough." has three camps for students wanting to immerse themselves in a basketball atmosphere; their camp at the University of Great Falls (Montana) offers both a day and overnight camp.

Plains States: In Minnesota, Bemidji State University offers boys, five different types of basketball camps, ranging from overnight to collegiate exposure; for girls, there's the option of either a day or overnight camp. For students that live farther south in the Plains States, Breakthrough Basketball's website lists a large variety of different camps in the Kansas City area - one is sure to be a fit for you.

Mississippi Valley: One of the biggest camps in this region, Missouri Rhythm, puts teaching young men spiritual and moral character on the same plane as learning how to play fundamental basketball. In Louisiana, La Salle College's camp is a strong one, as are the ones organized by Tennessee Tech.

Great Lakes Region: Ohio, birthplace of LeBron James, has a summer camp called the Cavaliers Youth Basketball Summer Camp. Sports-crazy Michigan also has strong selections, such as those offered by the Spartan Youth Programs and Northern Michigan University.

The Beginner's Guide to Becoming a Better Basketball Player

Northeast: In New York, eager high school students have an assortment of choices for camps: Hofstra University Summer Elite Basketball Camps and Potsdam Bears Summer Basketball Camp both teach kids invaluable fundamentals that'll better their skills. The Red Auerbach Basketball School in Rhode Island has been running successfully for over fifty years, and the All-Cape Hoop Camp in Cape Cod, Massachusetts is a great way for students to combine basketball training with a vacation atmosphere.

Mid-Atlantic: Keystone State Basketball Camp in Pennsylvania lists a multitude of camps for both boys and girls where they can learn under the tutelage of Pete White, a coach who's won seventeen District Championships in a row. In North Carolina, the state where I went to college, the East Carolina Boys' Basketball Camps are directed by Coach Lebo and tailored to different age and skill levels.

Southeast: This is my favorite region because this is where I live. If you live in this region, check out the Brian Gregory Basketball Camp at Georgia Tech for a place where you can train in small coach-to-student ratios and have the security of licensed collegiate trainers on hand. For students in Florida, Coach Marty's All Star Camps offer kids the chance to work on their basketball skills no matter what their talent levels are. I'm going to give a big shoutout to my Davidson guys, Brendan Winters and Logan Kosmalski. They recently started a youth basketball training program in the Charlotte, NC area called Pro Skills Basketball. These guys host camps, skill trainings, tournaments and more. NBA player Stephen Curry has partnered with the Accelerate Basketball Training group. He provides NBA skill trainings in Charlotte for all age groups.

Basketball Academy Benefits

"A winner is someone who recognizes their God given talents, works their tail off to develop them in to skills and uses these skills to accomplish their goals."

- Larry Bird

In my hometown, football was the dominant sport, even though I loved basketball. I loved the sport so much; I would have loved to have attended a school that dealt solely with it. Instead, I had to look up my own drills and work on them on my own time. In my personal story, I talked about how I didn't have much guidance and had to look up [Pete Maravich](#) and [Steve Nash's drills](#). At a [boarding school basketball academy](#), those drills would have already been put in place by seasoned coaches who would have known just what areas I should be targeting, without taking the focus off academics. I also would have loved to have seen how far I could push myself scholastically. In high school, I had a friend who played football. He wasn't the greatest football player and didn't break many records, but he ended up going to a football academy. As a result, he landed a scholarship to Virginia Tech and ended up becoming a NFL player for the Baltimore Ravens. As you can see, there are many benefits to attending a basketball academy in between high school and college:

- The concentration on basketball will help improve your skills quickly and immensely. Take ballet dancers, for example. They can spend their teen years at a normal high school, taking dance as a class or participating after school. However, to really improve, it's hard to argue with going to a school that focuses on hours of practice each day as part of the curriculum. LaSalle Academy in New York, NY is the alma mater of Metta World Peace (Ron Artest) and the only Hall of Fame pair of brothers, Dick and Al McGuire. This school is so intensely focused on basketball, playing in the gym has an atmosphere like a big city college game.

The Beginner's Guide to Becoming a Better Basketball Player

- The teaching staff are trained professionals in basketball. Some may be former NBA players that have wanted to give back, and some may be people who grew up surrounded by the sport. The coaches who'll help you with your game have years of dedicated experience in the game and can pick out your strengths and weaknesses in a flash.

- Scouts more often target academies. They see these schools as places specifically designed to develop basketball players and spend more of their time there. I'm not knocking regular schools because of their well-roundedness, but it's because of that that they might get left off the radar. Carmelo Anthony, Michael Beasley, Kevin Durant and Rajon Rondo all went to Oak Hill Academy, leading them to play at top-notch colleges where their play led them to being high draft picks in the NBA.

- The focus on academics may be more stringent. The teachers and coaches at basketball academies know that not every kid will reach the highest level, and so they prepare you thoroughly to succeed in all aspects of life. The best player in the NBA, LeBron James, went to St. Vincent-St. Mary High School, a place where the majority of students go on to get degrees, with a large portion of them attending on scholarships.

A formal basketball academy that you go to finish school might not be for you, but there are shorter academies available, such as summer camps. Some of the more known ones are the Kevin Durant Skills Academy Camp and the LeBron James Skills Academy. These are good because they give you a taste of what it's like to be away from home and in an atmosphere where you're surrounded by people, who live, breathe and sleep basketball. I loved my Davidson College experience, but coming out of high school, I wasn't highly recruited. If I could do it all over again, I would have went to a basketball academy to increase my scholarship opportunity.

WRITING FIRST BASKETBALL LETTER

"Love never fails, character never quits, and with patience and persistence, dreams do come true."

- Pete Maravich

If you decide not to go to a basketball academy, I'm going to teach you how to write college coaches and get their attention. When it comes time for you to decide which college you want to go to, there are many things to consider: tuition, location, academics, athletics, curricular activities, and the programs offered. If you're centering your college choice based on which school has the best basketball fit for you, one way of making an excellent first impression on prospective coaches is to write them a letter. I did this when I was applying to college, and received a reply from almost every coach that I wrote.

You may be thinking it'd be easier to make a phone call or write an email, and you'd be right. It is easier, but it's also lazy. It tells the coaches that you couldn't be bothered to take the time to organize all your information, sit down and write a letter, buy a postage stamp, and drop it in the mailbox. By writing a letter, you're telling them - without actually saying it - that you're willing to go one step further than everyone else. Coaches notice this, and they'll think, "If this student is willing to take the time to write a letter when it's absolutely not required, they're probably liable to take the time with other things in the game that matter."

Before you stop reading and go write that letter, take a few minutes to see what I put in my letter that got me a response from everyone. I started with the envelope because in my mind, it's the one piece that everyone forgets about until they've written the letter. On the front of the envelope, put the coach's name and address of the basketball department. For every school that you're

The Beginner's Guide to Becoming a Better Basketball Player

interested in, Google their websites and the address of each department should be there and easy to find. Beside the coach's name, write "ATTN" as in "ATTN: [Name]". This will ensure it gets to the right person. Next is the actual letter-writing process. Type the date in the top-left corner, then hit enter a few times and write in the coach's name, street address, and city/state/zip code, each on separate lines. Hit "enter" twice, and start the letter: "Dear Coach [Name]". The first paragraph should be used to introduce yourself. Tell the coach what school you go to and what year you're in, your height and weight, your role on the basketball team, and any and all awards you've won. You want to catch the coach's attention and keep him or her reading, so don't be shy in talking about yourself.

The second paragraph is where you get into more personal details, such as scholastic achievements. Start off the paragraph by mentioning the coach you currently play for, how to reach him or her, and the best way to get in contact with both of you (make sure to include your coach's contact information). Hopefully, you'll have been working hard at your studies, so mention your GPA (and what scale is used to measure it,) your SAT score (if you've taken the test,) any scholastic awards you've won or been nominated for, if you've taken any AP classes, where you rank in your class, and what program you want to study in college. Also, take a few lines to write why you're so interested in this particular college, as well as a line or two about their basketball program so it really appears as though you've researched the school and show a genuine intent in attending.

The third paragraph should be for mentioning that you've included a tape of you playing, how to recognize you, and what your basketball schedule is like for the upcoming year. Coaches are extremely busy and love anything that makes their lives easier; unless you have quite a reputation, they're also most likely not going to put everything down and rush out the door to see you play. Give them a chance to check out your skills beforehand and if they like what you have to offer, they have your schedule to come and watch you play or to send an assistant coach to scout you. However, make sure you pick the tape with care: tapes of exhibition games or pickup games at your local neighborhood court are not a good idea; tapes of high-level games where you're playing a good team featuring a skilled player being actively recruited by multiple colleges is an excellent idea.

The Beginner's Guide to Becoming a Better Basketball Player

The last paragraph is your sign-off paragraph. This is where you tell the coach that you'd be more than happy to provide him or her with any other information they'd need. End it off with a line that's hopeful and anticipatory, like, "I look forward to hearing from you." It's polite, and it puts the right kind of pressure on the coach to respond. Now that you've written an awesome letter that's sure to get you a response, the question of when to send it is a big one. Do it during the middle of the college basketball season and it'll most likely get ignored. It's just not a good time. Instead, wait until that college has played its last game - whether it's regular season or playoff - and send it then. As the team and coach wrap up everything that comes at season's end, it might sit on his or her desk for a couple of weeks, but there's a much better chance it'll be read with attention and interest. The off-season is when coaches have the most free time to both read your letter and watch the tape you've included, and they'll also be relaxed enough to send you a response.

The last thing you'd want is for your coach to read your letter after a particularly tough game and either ignore it or send you a two-line "No, thanks" letter. Prepare everything as fully as possible, really take the time to write a good letter - get someone to help you if your spelling or grammar isn't that great - and send it just as the off-season is about to begin. Don't stop here, there are other ways to help you get recruited as an athlete. Don't forget - things to include with the letter; highlight DVD, upcoming basketball schedule and academic transcript. Last but not least, make sure that if you tell a coach that you are going to follow-up via phone, you do exactly that, even if you have to leave a message.

The Beginner's Guide to Becoming a Better Basketball Player

SAMPLE LETTER TO COLLEGE BASKETBALL COACHES

Dear %Coach's Name%,

My name is %Your Name% from %City and State% and I play at %High School Name%. I am writing to you and your coaching staff because I am extremely interested in playing basketball at %College/University%. This has been a dream of mine since I was a kid.

I will be graduating from %High School Name% in %Year%. I know that I can be a contributor to your basketball program. I play %Basketball Position% for my high school and AAU (%AAU Team Name%) and am %Height% and %Weight%. Just to tell you a little bit about myself. As a high school student, I currently have a GPA of %GPA% and SAT score of %Score% (if applicable). (Put in some extracurricular activities if applicable). (Your academic strengths). (Say something about the college/University's academic record and your interest there).

(Include some upcoming plans, goals and basketball schedule in this paragraph). I hope that you are able to see me play. My head coaches' name is, %Coach's Name% and his contact information is %Coach's Email/Phone%. I have included a DVD which is my highlight video, upcoming basketball schedule and a copy of my academic transcript (if you have one).

I would love to meet you and talk about the possibility of being a part of your team in %Grad Year%. If there is anything I can do to help you decide whether I might be a good fit for your program, please don't hesitate to ask. I will follow up with you soon by phone and if you have any further questions, I look forward to answering them for you.

Thank you for your time and I look forward to hearing back from you.

Sincerely,

Lamar Hull - Student/Athlete

1234 Jordan Drive

Email: inspirationalbasketball20@gmail.com

Phone: 555-555-5555

Cell: 555-555-5555

The Beginner's Guide to Becoming a Better Basketball Player

10,000 HOURS RULE: BEGINNER TO EXPERT

"A lot of late nights in the gym, a lot of early mornings, especially when your friends are going out, you're going to the gym, those are the sacrifices that you have to make if you want to be an NBA basketball player."

– Jason Kidd

To be a good basketball player and chase your dreams, you have to put in the time. Author Malcolm Gladwell invented the 10,000 hours rules: to get really, really good at something, you have to put in ten-thousand hours of time spent on practicing your craft. Throughout high school, I worked out two hours each day for five days a week. Over four years, that worked out to be approximately two-thousand and eighty hours. That is a good start, and that was only high school. However, that wasn't enough!

One of my inspirations, Pete "Pistol" Maravich, sometimes practiced up to eight hours each day. Cedric Henderson, another hard worker that I look up to, says that he practiced up to five hours a day and took at least one-thousand shots. Stephen Curry, a player that I played with during my college years, spent countless hours perfecting his flip shot to get it where it is today. Even though he

The Beginner's Guide to Becoming a Better Basketball Player

has made it to the NBA, he still works on that shot, practicing it so intensely that he starts the drill over if he misses three times.

I'm not necessarily saying you have to practice X number of hours a day, or that X numbers of daily practice is guaranteed to get you into the NBA. What I am saying is that if you want to improve yourself and have a shot at achieving your dream, you have to roll up your sleeves and get dirty. Talent will only get you so far, but like so many athletes I saw in my hometown, it takes hard work, dedication and practice to carry you the rest of the way. Plus, by practicing with all you've got, you pick up valuable lessons along the way, like learning how mentally tough you are and what it takes to be a leader. All that time I spent practicing even in the off-season and how dedicated I was to helping our team get better is what impressed Coach Mckillop at Davidson. Ultimately, he was willing to make some calls for me so that I could [play professionally overseas](#).

Nobody has too much talent that they never have to practice or have nothing else to improve upon. Not even LeBron James. Jason Kidd said it best; you have to sacrifice your time to be great at something you love. How much time this week will you spend working on your game? Today, sit down and write your game plan!

MONDAY THROUGH FRIDAY WORKOUT PLAN

"Practice habits were crucial to my development in basketball. I didn't play against the toughest competition in high school, but one reason I was able to do well in college was that I mastered the fundamentals. You've got to have them down before you can even think about playing."

-Larry Bird

Working out was always really important to me for many reasons: I wasn't one of the flashiest or most-skilled guys on the court, so it gave me that extra edge to compete with them. Paying attention to conditioning also taught me the discipline and perseverance I needed to keep taking my game to the next level. Pushing myself through a set of AB crunches sometimes seemed like there was no point, that it had nothing to do with basketball, but looking back, it definitely had a direct impact on my being able to stay mentally and physically focused at the end of games.

On Mondays during the summer, the focus of my workout was shooting and lifting, interspersed with lifting weights. Wednesdays were fairly similar, but with an added focus on passing. There are hundreds of drills, exercises and workouts you could incorporate into your daily routine depending on what's good for you and the position you play, so to make it easier for you, I'll list the ones that worked best for me. Here is my Monday through Friday workout! This is just the foundation for you to get started, don't stop here, continue to build on this list or update it as needed for your specific position. Before jumping right in, ask yourself again, how bad do you want it? Will you continue to work out when you don't feel like it? Will you go hangout with your friends instead of working out? Will you be discipline enough to get the job done and get better day in and day out?

The Beginner's Guide to Becoming a Better Basketball Player

As an added bonus, you can do most of these drills inside or outside by yourself and a few of the drills will require a partner. Enjoy!

The Beginner's Guide to Becoming a Better Basketball Player

Monday (Shooting and Lifting) Workout

1. Check this article out on Inspirational Basketball that demonstrates the proper shooting technique! Don't skip this step because you will learn the best shooting mechanics before you start the shooting workout!

2. 5 minute LeBron James' AB workout Video

3. Warm-up (10 made free throws and stretch). Here are some warm-up stretches that you can use

4. Lay-ups
    - Layups from the right, middle and the left side of the rim
    - Start outside the 3 point line and drive to the rim
    - Perform the reverse layup from the left and right side
    - Note: layup with left hand, jump off the right foot. Layup with right hand, jump off the left foot. Flip the ball out, catch it off the bounce and then go!
    - Make all 5 layup options consecutively before moving to the next drill

5. One hand shooting drill
    - Shoot with one hand from the positions below with your shooting arm only
    - Make 5 shots in a row before moving to the next spot (bend your knees)
    - Note: Click on the One hand shooting drill video below for more instructions!

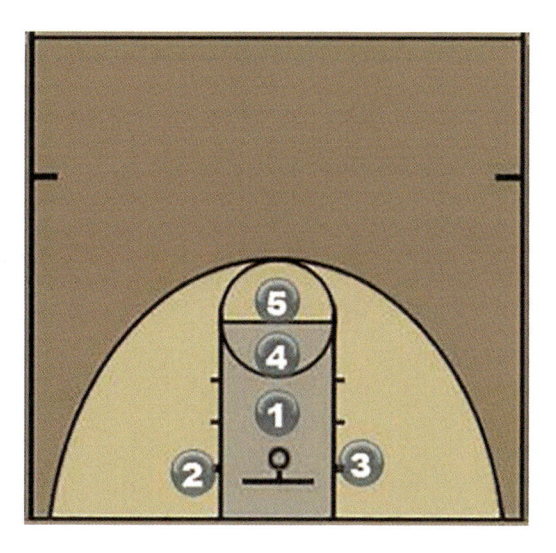

[One hand shooting drill video](#)

6. [Basketball Golf Drill](#)

    - Pre-select 9 positions inside the 3-point line

    - Shot from the first position until you have made the shot

    - Once you have made the shot, advance to the next spot

    - Use the backboard for any shots at a 45-degree angle

    - Stay in your shooting range and if you're comfortable, attempt 3 pointers

    - Ultimate goal is to complete this drill with 18 shots or less

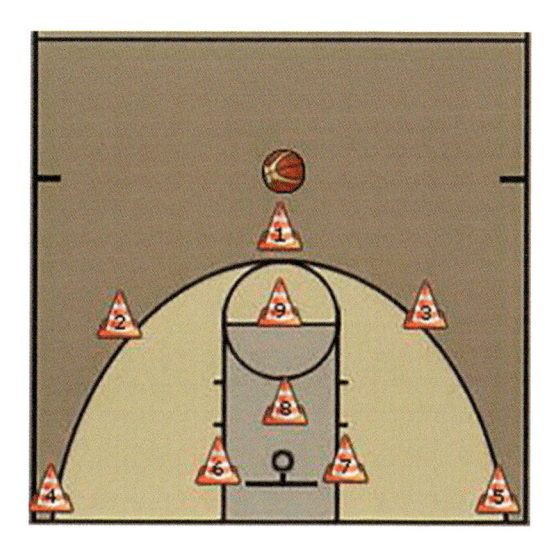

7. [Spot Shooting Drill](#)

- Pick 5 spots on the court and shoot 50 shots from each spot
- Spread the shots out and record your shooting percentage, so that you can get better each time you perform this drill

8. [Spot Shooting Drill 2](#)

- Flip the basketball out, catch the basketball on the bounce, square up and shoot
- Shoot anywhere inside the arc
- Do this for 7 minutes

9. Jump Shot off the Jap Step Series Drill

- Perform this drill from the top of the key
- Take a jab step, square up and shoot
- Take a jab step, then take one dribble to the right, and then take a jumper
- Take a jab step, then take 2 dribbles to the right, and then shoot a layup
- Don't move on until you make all 3 of these shots

10. Straight Shot Drill

- Perform this drill from the top of the key
- Flip the basketball out in front of you, step in to the shot and shoot
- Shoot 50 shots

11. Wing to Wing Drills

- You will need a partner *
- Run from elbow to elbow, receive the pass, square up on each shot, and then shoot
- Time yourself between 1-5 minutes (increase your time as you get better)

12. Crossover Floater Drill

- You will need a partner *
- Stand at the left elbow, run to the right elbow, receive the pass, crossover left-to-right into the lane, take one dribble and shoot a floater
- Leave your arm up as you shoot the floater until it drops in the net
- Perform this drill starting at the right elbow
- Make 10 floaters from each side

13. One-Two Dribbles Elbow Shot Drill

- Stand at the top of the key
- Swing through, one to two hard dribbles to the right elbow and shoot
- Alternate from right to left elbow
- Shoot 30-50 shots (shoot the same amount of shots from both elbows)

14. Distract the Shooter Drill

- You will need a partner *
- Stand at the top of the key
- Player 1 stands at the top of the key, player 2 stands on the baseline
- Player 2 throws a chest pass to Player 1
- Player 2 runs at Player 1 with a high hand and yelling at him or her to distract them
- Player 1 stands stationary and shoots the shot
- 10 made shots from each player

15. Distract the Shooter Drill 2

- Same as #15 but use a broom or a long object

16. Davidson Drills

- A partner may be needed for some of these drills*
- Each arrow describes a different drill, these are drills that I had to do in college in my individual workout
- Stand at the left corner of half court, swing through, take 1-2 dribbles and make the layup (5 made layups from both sides)
- Stand in the middle of half court, take 1-2 dribbles to the right elbow and take the jumper (5 made jumpers from both elbows)
- Stand at wing, swing through towards the baseline, take one dribble, crossover middle, and drive to the basket to make a layup (5 made layups from both wings)
- Shoot 3s non-stop around the arc for 3-5 minutes

The Beginner's Guide to Becoming a Better Basketball Player

- You are shooting from 3 spots x 5 (see below) – 3 pointer, 2 pointer and layup. Make your layup, shoot your mid-range shot, and then shoot a 3. You have to make all 3 shots before moving to the next station, if you miss one, start over at the same station with the layup

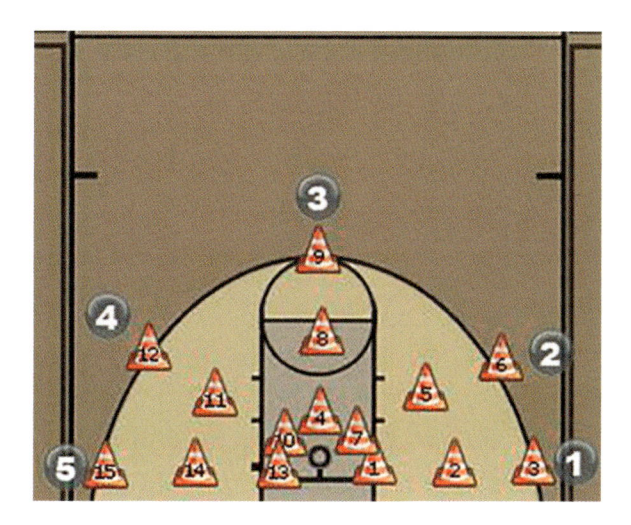

- Player 1 starts at the middle of half court, Player 2 stands at either wing, Player 1 drives to the elbow, Player 2 slides down towards the baseline, receives the pass and then shoots.

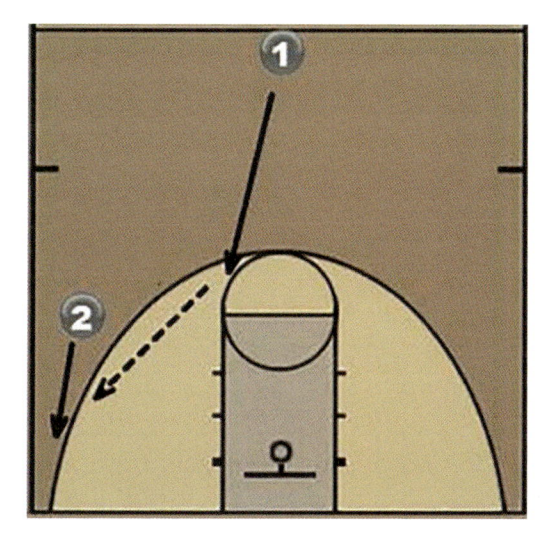

17. One on One Drill

- Player 2 starts on the block under the basket and rolls the ball out to Player 1 at the top of the key
- Player 2 touches the other block and then runs out and plays defense on Player 1
- The first player to 10 points wins with ever basket counting as 1 point. The game is make-it-take-it

18. One on One Spot Drill

- Player 1 stands under the basket and dribbles anywhere and puts the ball on the ground, player 2 follows and picks the ball up and gets in to a triple threat
- Player 2 performs the triple threat until Player 1 taps him or her and then they play one on one. Player 1 plays hard defense on Player 2 while he is in the triple threat
- The first to 10 points wins with ever basket counting as 1 point, and there are only 3 dribbles allowed

19. One on One Touch Drill

- Pick 9 spots around the perimeter
- Player 1 throws a chest pass to Player 2, Player 1 touches Player 2's hip and they play one on one
- The first player who scores from all 9 spots wins. The game is make-it-take-it

20. One on One Dribble Drill

- Player 1 throws a bounce pass to Player 2 who is spotted up in the corner behind the 3 point line
- Player 2 immediately tries to score, Player 1 forces Player 2 middle (force him to the defense)
- Perform this drill from both corners, the first to 5 from both corner wins, play make-it-take-it

21. V Cut Drill

- Set the ball on the wing, V cut and pick the ball up, swing through to the basket and perform the following scoring options
- Lay-up, Bank shot, Floater (make all shots from each wing in a row before moving on)
- Perform this drill from both wings

22. Step Back Drill

- Stand at the top of the key, dribble to the right elbow, perform the step back and then shot a jumper
- Score 10 times from both elbows

23. Foul Shooting

- Shoot 100 Free Throws

24. Warm-down (stretch)

25. Monday Weight Lifting (Chest)
    - Refer to weightlifting workout below

26. Nightly Dribbling Drills
    - Refer to dribbling drills on Tuesday

27. [5 minute AB Workout](#)

28. Work on shooting form lying on your back

Tuesday (Dribbling and Lifting) Workout

1. Run a Mile

2. Dribble in a Circle
    - Dribble in the half court circle for 5 minutes, performing a series of dribbling combinations
    - Keep your head up, change direction and pound the basketball

3. Finger Pad Control Drill

- Get on one knee and dribble with your fingertips
- Dribble 100 times with right hand, 100 times with left hand

4. Square V Dribble

- Each Dribble should perform a V motion
- 50 bounces for each type of V Dribble
- Front V Dribble (one hand – left and right/and 2 hands)
- Front In & Out Dribble (one hand – left and right)
- Side V Dribble (one hand – left and right)
- Between the Legs V Dribble (right leg in front, then left leg in front)
- Behind the Back V Dribble
- [Square V Dribble Video](#)

5. Walk with the Basketball

- Dribble high and dribble low
- Do this full court and back (low and high)

6. Run with the Basketball

- Dribble high and dribble low
- Do this full court and back (low and high)

7. Stop and Pop

- Perform this drill full court

- Take 3 full-speed dribbles, stop immediately and dribble as low as you can, do this for a few seconds and then take 3 more full-speed dribbles
- Repeat this process the full length of the court

8. Change Direction

- Perform this drill full court, down and back, full speed
- Change direction dribbling down the court, utilize the following moves
- Crossover, spin, between the legs, behind the back, and in & out crossover

9. Double Time

- Dribble the basketball slow while chopping your feet fast
- Perform this drill stationary with right and left hand
- 50 bounces (left and right hand)

10. Circle Dribble

- Sit Indian style; dribble the ball around you in a circular motion

11. Laid Back Drill

- Lay on your back and place your elbow on the floor
- Dribble the basketball with your fingertips without lifting your elbow off the floor
- Perform this drill with both left and right hand (50 bounces with both hands)

12. Figure 8 Dribble

- Dribble in a Figure 8 around both legs
- Small short dribbles
- Do this 10x without messing up
- Refer to this video on how to implement the Figure 8
- [Figure 8 Dribbling Video](#)

13. Circle Dribble Around One Leg

- Dribble the basketball around one leg in a circle, small short dribbles
- Perform this drill clockwise and counter clockwise
- Perform this drill around both legs – left leg, left hand and right leg, right hand
- 10x clockwise, 10x counter clockwise (left and right hand)

14. Squeeze the Banana

- Extend both arms above your head, hold the ball and squeeze it with your fingertips
- 15 squeezes with both hands, keep arms extended

15. Tap Drill

- Extend both arms above your head; tap the ball back and forth between fingertips (small taps)
- Keep arms extended, start from the top, small quick taps. Keep tapping and start moving your arms down until you stop at the bottom, keep arms extended and go up and down while tapping the basketball
- 10x (down and up counts as one rep)

The Beginner's Guide to Becoming a Better Basketball Player

16. Wall Tap Drill

    - Extend one arm and bounce the basketball off the wall (small taps, use fingertips)
    - 50x with each individual hand, 100x with both hands together

17. Pendulum Swing

    - Swing the ball like a pendulum swing and slap the ball each time you swing
    - it to the other hand
    - 50 slaps

18. Around the World

    - Circle the ball around your head (counter clockwise and clockwise) – 20x
    - Circle the ball around your waist (counter clockwise and clockwise) – 20x
    - Circle the ball around your legs (counter clockwise and clockwise) – 20x
    - Entire Body around the World
    - Circle the ball around your head, then your waist and then your legs
    - Go back and forth from your head down to your legs, then your legs back up to your head
    - Down and up is counted as 1, do this 20x

19. Pretzel

    - Hold the ball between your legs a few inches off of the ground
    - Place your right hand in the front and your left hand in the back; quickly switch your hands, with your left hand in the front and your right hand in the back.
    - Don't let the ball touch the ground, switch hands back and forth from the front to back. Perform 30 catches

20. Figure 8 in the Air

- Perform the figure 8 between your legs stationary, without letting the ball touch the ground
- Perform 20 full figure 8s

21. Figure 8 in the Air Walking

- Bend over and perform the figure 8 between your legs walking
- The basketball shouldn't touch the ground, up and down is counted as 1, perform 10 of these

22. Figure 8 in the Air Running

- Same concept as #21, you are just picking up your speed

23. Dribble with 2 Basketballs

- Dribble both basketballs with the same bounce (they should hit the ground at the same time. Perform 50 bounces!
- Dribble both basketballs with an alternate bounce (you should alternate when the basketballs hit the ground). Perform 100 bounces!
- Dribble one basketball high, dribble the other basketball low. Count 50 low bounces!

24. 35 Seconds Weak Hand Drill

- Dribble full court with weak hand, make a layup, dribble back with your weak hand, and make a layup
- Make 6 layups in 35 seconds

25. Spider Drill

    - Perform the spider drill

    - Refer to this [video to learn how to perform the spider drill](#)

26. Dribble with Eyes Close

    - Dribble for 10 minutes with eyes close

    - You should also [buy cheap basketball goggles](#) that you can use for this drill

27. Weight Lifting for Tuesdays (Legs)

    - Refer to weightlifting workout for each week

28. Nightly Dribbling Drills

    - Refer to dribbling drills on Tuesday

29. [5 minute AB Workout](#)

30. 100 push ups

Wednesday (Passing with a little Shooting) Workout

1. Run a Mile

2. [5 minute AB workout](#)

3. You can perform these drills with a partner or by yourself*

4. Rapid Fire Passing Drill
    - Chest pass to the wall starting real close, back up on every pass
    - Stop when the basketball can't reach you from bouncing it off the wall

5. Behind the Back Passing Drill
    - Behind the back pass to the wall without the ball touching the ground
    - Perform this drill with your left and right hand
    - 30 behind the back passes with your left and right hand each

6. Bounce Passing Drill
    - Bounce pass to the wall
    - 50 bounce passes

7. Over the head Passing Drill
    - Over the head pass to the wall
    - 50 passes

8. Over the head Fake Passing Drill

- Fake over the head, and then make a side one armed bounce pass to the wall
- 30 passes

9. Shoot 200 Shots

- Shoot 100, track how many you made
- Shoot 100, track how many you made. Try to beat the first 100 shots

10. 100 Free Throws

11. Wednesday Weightlifting (Back/Core)

- Refer to weightlifting workout

12. Nightly Dribbling Drills

- Refer to Dribbling Drills on Tuesday

13. [5 minute AB Workout](#)

14. 120 Pushups

15. Lay on your back and work on shooting form

Thursday (Defense with a little Shooting) Workout

1. Run a Mile

2. [5 minute AB Workout](#)

3. Tube Defensive Slide Drills
    - Step & Slide between the elbows
    - Perform at a slow pace, work on your technique
    - Stay low, back straight, feet shouldn't touch, and perform this drill for 1 minute

4. Defensive Slide Drills
    - Slide from elbow to elbow for 45 seconds

5. Deny Drill
    - Pretend that you are denying the ball on the wing for 45 seconds

6. COD Slide Drill
    - Change direction sliding down the court
    - Full speed down and back 5x

7. Close out Drill
    - Player 1 stands on the wing, player 2 starts under the basketball
    - Player 2 rolls the ball to player 1 and closes out top shoulder

- Player 2 sprints to Player 1 and as he/she gets close, short choppy steps with hand up
- Player 1 is trying to score
- Player 2 doesn't allow middle and beats Player 1 to the block if he drives
- Keys: short choppy steps on closeout, banana cut on closeout to force baseline, high hand on closeout, butt down and beat offensive player to the block if he/she drives
- If defense gets a stop, he/she goes on offense and if the offensive player scores, he/she stays on offense
- Player with 5 stops wins!

8. Defensive Cone Slide Drill
    - Put 2 cones elbow width apart
    - Slide back and forth and touch each cone
    - Time yourself for 1 minute and count each touch

9. Shoot 250 shots straight but in sets
    - Shoot 100, 100 and then 50
    - Shoot inside the arc

10. Rest and Lunch

11. Thursday Weightlifting (Upper Body - Arms)

12. Rest and Eat Dinner

13. Nightly Dribbling Drills
    - Refer to dribbling drills on Tuesday

14. [5 minute Abs workout](#)

15. 125 Push-ups

16. Lay down and work on shooting form

Friday (Conditioning with a little Shooting & Lifting) Workout

1. Run a Mile

2. [5 minute AB Workout](#)

3. Full Court Sprints
    - Down and back in 2 minutes
    - Count how many down and backs you get

4. Jumping Drills
    - Put feet close together, find a line, jump left to right for 30 seconds, jumping over the line
    - Jump forward and backwards – 1x
    - Jump east to west – 1x

5. Toe Touch Drill
    - Jump as high as you can and touch your toes
    - As soon as your feet touch the ground, jump as quick as you can
    - 30 seconds x1

6. Heel Touch Drill

    - Same as toe touch drill

7. Heel & Toe Touch Drill

    - Alternate heel and toe touch

    - Follow the same steps as #6 & #7

8. Slide Drill

    - Defensive slides from elbow to elbow

    - Go as hard as you can for 1 minute

9. Jump Stop Drill

    - Stand on the baseline, start sprinting and jump stop

    - Do this all the way to the other baseline

    - When you jump stop, work on your balance by having your feet shoulder width apart, arms out when you land

    - Sprint as hard as you can and get your balance as quick as you can when you jump stop

10. One Leg Drill

    - Jump 10x on left leg, jump 10x on right leg

    - Jump 30x off both legs

    - Perform this drill 3x

11. Kangaroo Jump

    - Take a step and jump off your right leg, land on your left leg

- Do this jumping off of your left let
- 10x both legs

12. Power Move Jump

    - Stand under the basket and try to touch the backboard with feet shoulder width a part
    - Once you land on the ground, side step and do the same thing on the other side of the backboard.
    - Get quicker each time and explode up to touch the backboard (if you can't touch the backboard, reach as high as you can) - Perform this drill for 60 seconds

13. Jump Rope Single Bounce

    - 10x, 20x, 30x
    - This is the regular jump rope

14. Jump Rope Single Speed Bounce

    - Try to get faster with your rope
    - 10x, 20x, 30x

15. Jump Rope Spread

    - Jump forward and backwards, feet together
    - 10x, 20x, 30x

16. Jump Rope Straddle

- Spread legs and then close them
- Alternate your legs by closing them and then shutting them, jump roping at the same time
- 10x, 20x, 20x

17. Jump Rope Double Jump

- Single jump, then double jump
- It doesn't matter if you keep messing up, keep trying
- Every time you complete a double jump that counts as 1 rep
- 5x, 10x, 15x

18. Jump Rope Side to Side

- Feet together, jump side to side
- 10x, 10x, 15x

19. Dribble the basketball from baseline to baseline

- Dribble with the least amount of dribbles
- Push the basketball
- 6x

20. Rest and Eat Lunch

21. Friday Weightlifting (Plyometrics)

22. Rest and Eat Dinner

23. Nightly Dribbling Drills
    - Refer to dribbling drills on Tuesday

24. [5 minute Abs workout](#)

Monday-Friday Conditioning & Weightlifting Workout

Remember to WARM UP and STRETCH before every workout! Rest for 20-60 seconds in between sets.

Monday – Upper Body (focus on Chest)

Dumbbell Bench Press – 2 Sets x 8-10 Reps

The dumbbell bench press is a great exercise for the upper body, primarily the chest. Basketball players will benefit from the increased upper body strength and stability gained from this exercise.

To perform the dumbbell bench press, simply lie down on a flat weight bench with two dumbbells of equal weight, one in each hand. Perform a bench press motion by pushing the dumbbells into the air and lowering them to your sides, this is one rep. You may use an inclined weight bench if you would like to incorporate the shoulder muscles more.

Dumbbell Fly – 3 Sets x 8-10 Reps

The dumbbell fly is a good exercise to strengthen the chest muscles, as well as the shoulders. Basketball players will benefit from the increased upper body strength and stability gained from this exercise.

The perform a dumbbell fly, lie down on a flat weight bench holding a dumbbell in each hand. Then hold the dumbbells straight above your chest while keeping your elbows slightly bent. Next, lower the dumbbells straight out to your sides; the movement should look like a bird flapping its wings. When you bring the dumbbells back up above your chest, you have completed one rep.

Tuesday – Legs

Weighted Walking Lunge – 2 Sets x 15-20 Reps

Leg strength and endurance is necessary for a basketball player. Walking lunges will help prepare your legs for running back and forth on the hardwood basketball court.

To perform the walking lunge, simply load up your weight (place a barbell over your shoulders or carry a kettlebell/dumbbell in each hand) and step forward. When you step forward, bend down and drop your rear knee until it almost touches the floor. Make sure your front knee is bent so that your leg makes a 90 degree angle. To complete each rep, bring your rear leg forward and bend down again, you should end up 'walking' forwards as you complete the set. You may perform the lunges in place if you do not have enough room.

Weighted Calf Raise – 3 Sets x 8-10 Reps

Many athletes either completely ignore or under-develop the calf muscles of the legs. Weighted calf raises are the perfect exercise for strengthening the calf muscles which are a key muscle used in both running and jumping.

To perform a weighted calf raise, load up your desired weight (place a barbell over your shoulders or carry a kettlebell/dumbbell in each hand) and stand with your feet shoulder-width apart. Next, raise up your heels (standing on your toes) and hold the position for about two seconds, then lower back down; this is one rep.

Wednesday – Back / Core

Bent-Over Row – 2 Sets x 8-10 Reps

The bent-over row targets the middle back while also strengthening the upper back and shoulders. It is a good exercise to increase the strength and stability of the trunk of the body.

The bent-over row requires a barbell (or two dumbbells). Stand with your feet shoulder-width apart; you may offset one foot to the front or back for stability. Lift up the barbell with your palms facing down in front of you and bend your back forwards at about a 30-45 degree angle. While keeping your back bent, lower the barbell in front if you and lift it back up to your chest in a rowing motion; this is one rep.

Deadlift – 2 Sets 8-10 Reps

The deadlift is a classic power-lifting exercise that works extremely well for strengthening the important muscles of the lower back.

To perform a deadlift, place a loaded barbell on the ground directly in front of you. Bend your knees (so that they are above the bar) and grab the bar with your hands outside of your knees. Stand up, lifting the barbell using your back. Make sure to keep your back straight; this is one rep.

Front and Side Plank – 2 Sets x 45-60 Seconds Each

Planks are a good exercise to increase both core strength and stability. Basketball players need core stability to perform at a high level, which makes the safe-and-easy plank exercises perfect for basketball players.

To perform a front plank, assume a push-up position. Lower your elbows to the ground, creating a 90 degree angle with your arms. Your forearms should be on the ground. Hold this position for about one minute. To perform a side plank, lie down on your side, then lift your upper body up using your forearm; your upper arm should make a 90 degree angle with your torso. Perform the side plank on each side.

Thursday – Upper Body (focus on Arms)

Hammer Curl – 2 Sets x 8-10 Reps (per arm)

Hammer curls are a perfect exercise for strengthening both the forearms and biceps, as opposed to regular curls which target only the bicep muscles.

To perform a hammer curl, stand with your feet shoulder-width apart with your hands at your sides, a dumbbell in each hand. While keeping your palms facing each other and your elbows at your sides, lift the dumbbells up until your arm makes a 90 degree angle, then lower the weights; this is one rep. You may alternate arms.

Triceps Extension – 2 Sets x 8-10 Reps (per arm)

The triceps extension is an easy way to strengthen the triceps muscle using a dumbbell.

To perform a triceps extension, begin by holding a dumbbell behind your head using both hands. Hold onto the end of the dumbbell; your elbows should be up in the air. Lift the dumbbell straight up into the air by straightening out your arms. To complete the rep, lower the weight back down into the starting position.

Shoulder Press – 2 Sets x 8-10 Reps

The actions of throwing and shooting a basketball recruit the shoulder muscles more than anything else. The shoulder press is a simple exercise that uses dumbbells to strengthen the shoulder muscles.

To perform a shoulder press, hold up a dumbbell in each hand beside your head. With your palms facing the front, push the dumbbells straight up into the air and lower; this is one rep.

Friday – Plyometrics

Plyometric Push-up – 3 Sets x 8-10 Reps

The plyometric push-up is the perfect body-weight exercise for developing an explosive upper body.

To perform a standard plyometric (or clap) push-up, assume the push-up position. After lowering your chest to the ground, explode upwards into the air. While in the air, clap your hands together before landing; this is one rep.

Squat Jump – 2 Sets x 8-10 Reps

In a sport where jumping is almost as frequent as throwing, developing explosive legs is necessary. Squat jumps will increase your vertical jump.

To perform a squat jump, stand with your feet shoulder-width apart. Bend your knees and squat down until your bottom is level with your knees, then leap straight up as high as you can; this is a single rep.

Bounding – 2 Sets x 8-10 Reps

Bounding is a good complementary exercise to the squat jump that will further exercise your lower body.

To perform the bounding exercise, stand with your feet slightly more than shoulder-width apart. Jump as far as you can forwards, landing in the same position; this is one rep. Perform each bound with no more than a second of rest in between.

Notes/Tips

- Make sure to stay hydrated throughout your exercises.

- Practice proper technique before using heavy weights.

- When lifting weights, perform the reps at a fast pace, as this will work your fast twitch muscle fibers more. If your exercises are slow, you will become slow.

- Use a spotter whenever necessary.

- Try to increase your weight on each rep.

- Increase the amount of reps as you get stronger.

- Focus on speed, use light weight when starting out.

- Find other weightlifting exercises that you can use.

CONCLUSION

There's no one routine that will work for everyone, but the main thing to keep in mind is that basketball is a running game. You'll need endurance, but you'll also need to be able to turn on the jets for a quick breakout. Along with that, quick reflexes and being able to pivot on a dime require flexibility and grace, two components you shouldn't ignore at the expense of brute strength.

Also, keep in mind that switching up your routine will be easier on your body over the long-term. Not only will doing different routines on different days keep your body from getting used to the exercise, but it can also help prevent repetition injuries, one of the easiest types of injuries to avoid just by taking precautions.

The exercises that I incorporated into my routine, may not work for you. You might choose to take a few of the things that I practiced with and mix it into your own basketball routine. Learn some of the best scoring strategies and fundamentals so that you can be unguardable. Use your inner passion and strive to be great at whatever you do. The ultimate goal of this eBook and inspirationalbasketball.com is to inspire basketball players to be great and follow their dreams! I hope you have enjoyed reading this eBook and found it useful. Visit my inspirationalbasketball.com or email me at inspirationalbasketball20@gmail.com and leave a testimony so that I can add it to the website. Thanks again for reading and I can't wait to hear about your success!

RESOURCES

http://inspirationalbasketball.com/

www.amazon.com/gp/product/b000a7ovo4/ref=as_li_qf_sp_asin_tl?ie=utf8&camp=211189&creative=373489&creativeasin=b000a7ovo4&link_code=as3&tag=inspiryouthba-20

ebh.effectiveballhandling.com/wordpress/?page_id=207

www.amazon.com/gp/product/b000vnmmy8/ref=as_li_qf_sp_asin_il_tl?ie=utf8&camp=1789&creative=9325&creativeasin=b000vnmmy8&linkcode=as2&tag=inspiryouthba-20

inspirationalbasketball.com/pistol-pete-maravich/

http://instantoffense.com/?hop=0

http://www.teamgarnettbasketball.com/

www.amazon.com/gp/product/b000a7ovo4/ref=as_li_qf_sp_asin_tl?ie=utf8&camp=211189&creative=373489&creativeasin=b000a7ovo4&link_code=as3&tag=inspiryouthba-20

www.reachingtherim.com/

http://unguardablevolume1.com/?hop=0

www.davidsonwildcats.com/coaches.aspx?rc=596&path=mbball

yourbasketballtraining.com/products/thepointguardacademy/?hop=lahull20

inspirationalbasketball.com/should-your-child-play-multiple-sports/

inspirationalbasketball.com/playing-aau-or-yboa-youth-basketball/

inspirationalbasketball.com/how-to-earn-a-college-basketball-scholarship/

stephencurry30.com/

www.amazon.com/gp/product/B00HH9QU1A/ref=as_li_tl?ie=UTF8&camp=1789&creative=9325&creativeASIN=B00HH9QU1A&linkCode=as2&tag=inspiryouthba-20&linkId=FT4HLQZ74APTAXOR

inspirationalbasketball.com/guide-to-playing-professional-basketball-overseas/

www.youtube.com/watch?v=d-cg0wdb8ui

www.aauboysbasketball.org/

yboa.org/

rcbahoops.com

www.amazon.com/gp/product/b000vnmmy8/ref=as_li_qf_sp_asin_il_tl?ie=utf8&camp=1789&creative=9325&creativeasin=b000vnmmy8&linkcode=as2&tag=inspiryouthba-20

www.socalhoops.com/

eliteleaguebasketball.com/

www.breakthroughbasketball.com/camps/

www.amazon.com/gp/product/0316017930/ref=as_li_qf_sp_asin_tl?ie=utf8&camp=1789&creative=9325&creativeasin=0316017930&linkcode=as2&tag=inspiryouthba-20

www.missourirhythm.com/

www.nba.com/cavaliers/hoops/camps

superhoopcamps.com/

superhoopcamps.com/ac/home.htm

martyscamps.com/

proskillsbasketball.com/

www.acceleratebasketball.com/index.php/camps/sc30camps

www.boardingschoolreview.com/boarding_schools_sports/sport/1

articles.philly.com/2011-06-04/sports/29621024_1_summer-courses-scholarships-maine-central-institute

www.positionsports.com/kevin-durant-skills/

www.positionsports.com/lebron-james-skills/

www.amazon.com/gp/product/1932662995/ref=as_li_qf_sp_asin_il_tl?ie=UTF8&camp=1789&creative=9325&creativeASIN=1932662995&linkCode=as2&tag=inspiryouthba-20&linkId=GWSI5HJFESXSUGHO

inspirationalbasketball.com/guide-to-playing-professional-basketball-overseas/

inspirationalbasketball.com/10-basketball-shooting-techniques-that-will-increase-your-shooting-percentage-by-20-percent/

www.youtube.com/watch?v=kyerbk1lune

inspirationalbasketball.com/youth-basketball-stretches/

www.youtube.com/watch?v=_kmxwryx8s8

inspirationalbasketball.com/basketball-golf-shooting-drill/

inspirationalbasketball.com/spot-shooting-basketball-drill/

inspirationalbasketball.com/how-to-shoot-a-basketball-floater-tear-drop-runner/

inspirationalbasketball.com/v-dribbling-drill/

inspirationalbasketball.com/figure-8-dribbling-drill/

inspirationalbasketball.com/spider-dribbling-drill/

www.amazon.com/gp/product/B0000BYS19/ref=as_li_qf_sp_asin_il_tl?ie=UTF8&camp=1789&creative=9325&creativeASIN=B0000BYS19&linkCode=as2&tag=inspiryouthba-20&linkId=SPL5E6VUEEBG5GEX

http://www.amazon.com/gp/product/B003QHZ1YE/ref=as_li_tl?ie=UTF8&camp=1789&creative=9325&creativeASIN=B003QHZ1YE&linkCode=as2&tag=inspiryouthba-20&linkId=YADNHZRM7KQ62F2S

http://inspirationalbasketball.com/basketball-camps/

Printed in Great Britain
by Amazon